Jackdaws Anthologies

Pack 2

Gill Howell

Teaching Notes

Curriculum coverage chart 3

Dragon Fights
Reading 6
Comprehension 8
Speaking and listening 8
Writing 8

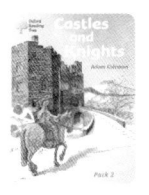

Castles and Knights
Reading 9
Comprehension 11
Speaking and listening 11
Writing 11

Seeds and Grain
Reading 12
Comprehension 14
Speaking and listening 14
Writing 14

Haunted Houses
Reading 15
Comprehension 17
Speaking and listening 17
Writing 17

Seas and Storms
Reading 18
Comprehension 20
Speaking and listening 20
Writing 20

Games and Races
Reading 21
Comprehension 23
Speaking and listening 23
Writing 23

Links to other Oxford Reading Tree titles 24

Introduction

Jackdaws Anthologies extend competent readers by providing different text types, including modern stories, traditional tales and non-fiction texts linked by a common theme. They are suitable for children working towards NC level 3/5–14 level C.

It is still important to introduce the story through discussion, to enable children to read the texts with increasing confidence and independence.

The sight vocabulary the children have gained in the earlier stages provides a platform for children to combine their knowledge of letter sounds and word meanings to interpret new words as they meet them in these stories.

Words from the NLS high frequency word list for Years 1 to 2 are also used, so children can reinforce their knowledge of them.

How to introduce the books

Introducing the stories and texts before independent reading is important in order to give the children sufficient information about the context and setting to enable them to read confidently and independently.

Before reading the text, talk about the front cover and the title. Read the back cover blurb and ask them to predict what the story or text is about. Go through the book together, looking at the pictures and talking about them. Point out and read any new context words that might prove difficult.

This booklet provides suggestions for using the books in group and independent reading activities. Prompts and ideas are provided for introducing and reading each book with a child or group of children.

Suggestions are also provided for writing, speaking and listening, and cross-curricular links. You can use these suggestions to follow on from your reading, or use them at another time.

Guided Reading Cards are available for each book. These provide ideas for taking a guided reading session.

Take-Home Cards are also available for each book. These provide friendly prompts and suggestions for parents reading with their children. You can store the relevant card with each book in your "Take-Home" selection of titles.

Vocabulary chart

	**DRAGON FIGHTS**
Karen's Adventure	
Years 1 to 2 High frequency words	after again an as back be been but by can't could did do don't door down first from got had has have her him his house how if just little live made make may more much must next night not now off old once one or out over put saw should so some that them then time there to took tree us very way were what when where will with would your
Context words	greenhouse lightning mirror orchard
All About Dragons	
Years 1 to 2 High frequency words	about people
Context words	camel demon stag
Hott's First Dragon	
Years 1 to 2 High frequency words	because boy called came help man many pull who
Context words	Bothva coward Denmark monsters Norway trembling warriors whimpering
	**CASTLES AND KNIGHTS**
The Playroom	
Years 1 to 2 High frequency words	about after another as be bed been but by came could did do door down first from got had have her here him his home house how if just made make may more must new next not now off once one out over put saw seen should so some take than that their them then there three time too two us very want way were what when where who will with your
Context words	castle courtyard disguise knights prisoner rescue surrender
Castles	
Years 1 to 2 High frequency words	an called dig lived many people water would
Context words	Celts Romans Motte and Bailey Normans siege
The Ghostly Battle	
Years 1 to 2 High frequency words	back laugh night
Context words	Cambridge ghostly Wandlebury warrior
	**SEEDS AND GRAIN**
Kate's Garden	
Years 1 to 2 High frequency words	about again as back be bed been but called came can't did dig do don't down first from had has have her how if just little make more much must next not now our out over put school should sister some take than that their them then there these time too two very want water were what when will with your
Context words	lettuce marigolds pansies patient sunflower tomato vegetable
All About Seeds	
Years 1 to 2 High frequency words	an help made many may once so where
Context words	germinate moisture
The Wise Chicken	
Years 1 to 2 High frequency words	after another could good old took us who would
Context words	loaf wheat
The Gift of Corn	
Years 1 to 2 High frequency words	because by here him home live lived man name night people pull saw
Context words	Canada chief cornfield plume tribe wrestle

HAUNTED HOUSES	
William and the Ghost	
Years 1 to 2 High frequency words about again an as back be because bed been but called came can't could did do don't door down first good had has have here his house how if jump just little live love made make man much must now off old one or our out over people put ran saw school seen sister so some that them there time too took two very want way were what when where will with	
Context words armour battlements ghost moat monastery treasure	
All About Ghosts	
Years 1 to 2 High frequency words not who	
Context words haunted theatre	
Miss Terry's Holiday	
Years 1 to 2 High frequency words after another by girl half help her him home many next should would your	
Context words cottage garage hedgerows meadow mechanic sandwiches telephone	
SEAS AND STORMS	
Danger at Sea	
Years 1 to 2 High frequency words about again another as back be been boy but by came can't could do don't down first from good got had have help her him his house if just little live love made man may name not now off one or our out over pull put ran saw should so some take that their then there time too took two us very way were what when where who will with would your	
Context words amusement arcade dodgems lifeboat lifeguard	
All About Lighthouses	
Years 1 to 2 High frequency words after make many must night them these	
Context words Boulogne lighthouses lightvessels Switzerland	
Grace Darling	
Years 1 to 2 High frequency words bed brothers called did half home how last people school sisters want	
Context words Forfarshire lighthouse passengers	
GAMES AND RACES	
The Catch	
Years 1 to 2 High frequency words about after an as back ball be because been but by called came can't could did do don't down first from girls got had have help her him his if just last little made make may more much next not now one our out over pull put ran saw school seen so some take than that their then there three time too two very want way were what when where who will with would your	
Context words baseball miserable rounders substitute wheelchair	
Chinese Horoscopes	
Years 1 to 2 High frequency words love	
Context words horoscopes intelligent mischief patience stubborn	
The Race	
Years 1 to 2 High frequency words again homes live lived must new old should them water	
Context words argument creatures emperor procession	

Curriculum coverage chart

	Speaking and listening	Reading	Writing
Dragon Fights			
Scotland	Level B	Level B	Level B
N.Ireland	Activities: a, d, e, f Outcomes: a, b, c, d, e	Activities: a, d, f, h, j Outcomes: a, g, h,	Outcomes: b, c,
Wales	Range:1, 4, 5 Skills: 1, 2, 4, 5	Range: 1, 3, 5, 6 Skills: 1, 2, 4, 7, 8	Range: 1, 3, Skills:
NLS/NC	3a	W19, S1, S4, S6, T3, T8, T17	T9
Castles and Knights			
Scotland	Level B	Level B	Level B
N.Ireland	Activities: a, d, e, Outcomes: a, b, d	Activities: a, c, g, h, i, Outcomes: a, g, h, k	Outcomes: a, c, d, e, k
Wales	Range: 1, 5, Skills: 1, 2, 6	Range: 1, 3, 5, 6 Skills: 1, 2, 4, 5, 7, 8	Range: 1, 3, 5 Skills: 4, 5, 6
NLS/NC	4a, 4b, 4c	W4, S1, S7, T1, T2, T17, T21	T11
Seeds and Grain			
Scotland	Level B	Level B	Level B
N.Ireland	Activities: a, h Outcomes: b, d, e, g	Activities: a, c, e, f, h Outcomes: a, g, h, k	Outcomes: b, c, f
Wales	Range: 1, 2 Skills: 1, 2	Range: 1, 5, 6 Skills: 1, 2, 4, 5, 7, 8	Range: 1, 3, 4 Skills: 1, 2, 3, 5, 6
NLS/NC	1d, 1e	W1, W19, S1, S4, S7, T1, T5, T17, T18	T23
Haunted Houses			
Scotland	Level B	Level B	Level B
N.Ireland	Activities: a, d, e, f Outcomes: a, c, d	Activities: a, b, c, f, h Outcomes: a, g, k	Outcomes: a, c, d, f
Wales	Range: 1, 4 Skills: 1, 2, 7	Range: 1, 2, 3, 5, 7 Skills: 1, 2, 3, 4, 5, 7	Range: 1, 3, 5 Skills: 1, 5, 6
NLS/NC	3a, 3c	W8, S1, S3, S13, T1, T8, T17	T11
Seas and Storms			
Scotland	Level B	Level B	Level B
N.Ireland	Activities: a, b, d, e, f Outcomes: a, b, d	Activities: a, b, c, d, f Outcomes: a, g, h, i	Outcomes: a, c, d, f
Wales	Range: 1, 4, 5 Skills: 1, 2, 6	Range: 1, 3, 5, 6 Skills: 1, 2, 3, 4, 7	Range: 1, 3, 4, 5 Skills: 1, 2, 4, 5, 7
NLS/NC	2b, 2e, 4c	W4, S2, S4, T2, T17, T3, T4, T14	T19
Games and Races			
Scotland	Level B	Level B	Level B
N.Ireland	Activities: a, b Outcomes: c, d	Activities: a, b, c, f, h, Outcomes: a, g, h, k	Outcomes: a, d, f
Wales	Range: 1, 3, 4, 5, 6 Skills: 1, 2, 6	Range: 1, 3, 4, 5, 6 Skills: 1, 2, 4, 7	Range: 1, 3, 4, 5 Skills: 1, 4, 5, 6
NLS/NC	3a, 3e	W7, S2, S3, S4, T1, T2, T17	T11

Dragon Fights

Before reading

- Look at the front cover with the children and read the title together. Flick through the book and talk about how this is an anthology, with more than one story, unlike many other Oxford Reading Tree books they have read.
- Ask the children to flick through the book and talk together about the three texts it contains. Ask the children: *What links these texts?* (dragons) *What is the main difference?* (Two are stories, one is non-fiction.)

During reading

- Ask the children to read **Karen's Adventure, All About Dragons**, and **Hott's First Dragon** on separate occasions. Vocabulary that children may need help with includes "comfortable" p14; "mirrors" p16; "reflection" p20; "fierce" p24; "Bothva", "whimpering" p25; "plunged" p30. Praise and encourage them while they read. Prompt as necessary.

Observing Check that the children:
- understand the distinction between fact and fiction (Y3T1 T17)
- use a range of strategies to decipher new or unfamiliar words (Y3T1 S1).

Group and independent reading activities

Text level work

Objective To express their views about a story, identifying specific words or phrases to support their viewpoint (Y3T1 T8).

- Ask the children to compare the settings of **Karen's Adventure** and **Hott's First Dragon**. Ask: *In which story would you least expect to find a dragon?* (**Karen's Adventure** has an everyday setting.) Ask them to find words in the text to support their view. ("It was the first day of the holidays;" "Gran's house was in the country;" "Long, long ago, when monsters roamed the Earth.")

Observing Are the children able to identify words that show an everyday setting and the setting of a fantasy or legend?

Objective To be aware of the different voices in stories using dramatised readings, showing differences between the narrator and different characters used (Y3T1 T3).

- Ask the children to work in threes and take the roles of narrator, Hott and Bothva. Tell them to read pages 26–30, noting the verbs used in reported speech and reading with expression appropriate to each character.

Observing Do the children use the punctuation and grammar to help them read with expression?

Objective To understand the difference between fact and fiction; to use terms "fact", "fiction" and "non-fiction" appropriately (Y3T1 T17).

- Ask the children to look at the text on pages 22 and 23. Ask: *How does this text differ from the rest of the anthology?* (non-fiction) Ask them to describe some of the features that show the difference (present tense verbs, plurals, generalised nouns, photographs).

Observing Do the children use the term "non-fiction"?

Sentence level work

Objective To secure knowledge of question marks and exclamation marks in reading, understand their purpose and use appropriately in own writing (Y3T1 S6).

- Ask the children to find the questions on pages 22 and 23. Ask: *How do the questions begin and end?* Ask: *What is the consistent feature?* (They all end with a question mark.) Ask them to find other examples of punctuation used to end sentences (full stops, exclamation mark).

Observing Do the children note that a colon is used before the list of description, not a full stop, exclamation mark or question mark?

Objective To use verb tenses with increasing accuracy in speaking and writing. Use past tense consistently for narration (Y3T1 S4).

- Ask the children to work with a partner and take turns to re-tell each story using their own words.

Observing Do the children keep to the past tense while re-telling, e.g. "He went" instead of "He goes"?

Dragon Fights

Word level work

Objective To extend common vocabulary for introducing and concluding dialogue. Collect examples from reading (Y3T1 W19).

- Ask the children to collect examples of verbs used in reporting clauses from **Hott's First Dragon**. Ask: *How do the verbs affect the way you read the dialogue?*

Observing Do the children scan the text to find where speech marks indicate dialogue, helping them find the verbs easily?

Comprehension

Ask the children:
- *Why did the dragon climb through the kitchen window?* (p17 He was looking for food.)
- *Why does Karen's dragon change into a fierce red dragon?* (p17 Because he eats chicken.)
- *In which country do people think dragons make it rain?* (p22 China)
- *What did Hott do that made him feel brave?* (p30 He tasted dragon's blood.)

Speaking and listening activities

Objective Make contributions relevant to the topic and take turns in discussion (3a).

- Discuss Karen, Bothva and Hott's reactions to meeting dragons. Ask each child: *How would you feel if you met a dragon?*

Writing

Objective To generate ideas relevant to a topic by brainstorming, word association, etc. (Y3T1 T9).

- Ask the children to look at the descriptions of dragons in the three texts. Create a class spidergram of descriptive vocabulary for a dragon.

◀▶ **Cross-curricular link**
Design and Technology: moving monsters

Castles and Knights

Before reading

- Look at the front cover with the children and read the title together. Flick through the book and talk about how this is an anthology, with more than one story, unlike many other Oxford Reading Tree books they have read.
- Ask the children to flick through the book and talk together about the three texts it contains. Ask the children: *What links these texts?* (castles) *What is the main difference?* (Two are stories, one is non-fiction.)

During reading

- Ask the children to read *The Playroom*, *Castles* and *The Ghostly Battle* on separate occasions. Vocabulary that children may need help with includes "knights" p6; "neighing" p8; "disguise" p10; "kneel" p22; "Wandlebury" p28; "mysterious", "magnificent" p31. Praise and encourage them while they read. Prompt as necessary.

Observing Check that the children:

- understand the distinction between fact and fiction (Y3T1 T17)
- use a range of strategies to make sense of what they read (Y3T1 S1).

Group and independent reading activities

Text level work

Objective To comprehend how dialogue is presented in stories; how paragraphing is used to organise dialogue (Y3T1 T2).

- Ask the children to re-write the dialogue from pages 4 and 5 of *The Playroom* on to separate cut-out strips of paper. Tell them to rearrange the dialogue into sequence to show where it changes from one character to another.

Observing Do the children understand that a new character's speech needs a new line?

Objective To read information passages, and identify main points or gist of text (Y3T1 T21).

- Ask the children to read *Castles*. Tell them to make four columns on a piece of paper, and list two key facts for each type of castle in the columns.

Observing Do the children identify where the text changes from one period to the next to enable them to find two key points for each?

Objective To compare a range of story settings, and select words and phrases that describe scenes (Y3T1 T1).

- Ask the children to scan the two stories, **The Playroom** and **The Ghostly Battle**, and collect examples of descriptive words in both stories. Ask: *Which story uses the most descriptive vocabulary? Do the illustrations help to set the scene?*

Observing Do the children differentiate between description in the text and in the illustrations?

Sentence level work

Objective To observe the basic conventions of speech punctuation (Y3T1 S7).

- Write these examples of speech from **The Playroom** on the board or paper.
  > Are these all your toys? asked Jo.
  > Not all of them said Great-grandfather. Some were my grandfather's.
  > They're wonderful gasped Jo. Do you still play with them?
  > Every day replied Great-grandfather.
  > Do you have a favourite? asked Jo.
  > Oh yes said Great-grandfather, come and see.
- Ask the children to fill in the missing punctuation.

Observing Do the children open and close the spoken words with speech marks, and use commas before the reporting clause?

Word level work

Objective To discriminate syllables in reading and spelling (Y3T1 W4).

- Write the word "Wandlebury" on the board. Ask the children to clap the number of syllables in this word (four syllables). Remind them that syllables are the "beats" in a word, not the number of letters or phonemes.
- Ask the children to skim-read the story of **The Ghostly Battle** and write down any other words with four or more syllables (mysterious, everybody, magnificent). Early finishers could list words with three syllables (warrior, provided, champion, excitement, galloping, quietly, anyone, nobody).

Castles and Knights

Observing Do the children skim the text to find the four-syllable words?

Comprehension
Ask the children:
- *Why did Jo go into the playroom at night?* (p8 Because she heard noises.)
- *Did the castle grow bigger, or Jo grow smaller? How do you know?* (Jo grew smaller. p9 She was no bigger than a toy soldier. On p11 the paint box was bigger than she was.)
- *Why did people build castles?* (p27 to protect themselves from their enemies)
- *Is the legend of* **The Ghostly Battle** *fiction or non-fiction? Give evidence from the text to support your answer.* (p28 fiction, because it is told as a story, e.g. "One bitter winter's evening")

Speaking and listening activities

Objectives Create, adapt and sustain different roles, individually and in groups (4a); use character, action and narrative to convey story (4b); use dramatic techniques to explore characters and issues (4c).

- Ask children to take turns to sit in the "hot-seat" and take the roles of Sir Osbert, or Sir Osbert's friend.
- Ask the other children to ask questions about the legend of **The Ghostly Battle**.

Writing

Objective To develop the use of settings in own stories by writing a description in the style of a familiar story (Y3T1 T11).

- Ask the children to read **The Ghostly Battle**, and to write a description of the Wandlebury Hill using their own words.

◀▶ **Cross-curricular link**
History: Why have people invaded and settled in Britain in the past? A Roman case study

Castles and Knights   11

Seeds and Grain

Before reading

- Look at the front cover with the children and read the title together. Flick through the book and talk about how this is an anthology, with more than one story, unlike many other Oxford Reading Tree books they have read.
- Ask the children: *What links these texts?* (seeds topic) *What sort of texts does the anthology contain?* (a story in a modern setting, a non-fiction report, a traditional tale and a myth)

During reading

- Ask the children to read the texts on separate occasions. Vocabulary that children may need help with includes "lettuce", "patient" p9; "moisture", "germinate" p18; "delicious" p24; "wrestle" p29. Praise and encourage them while they read. Prompt as necessary.

Observing Check that the children:
- understand the difference between fiction and non-fiction (Y3T1 T17)
- use awareness of grammar to decipher new or unfamiliar words (Y3T1 S1).

Group and independent reading activities

Text level work

Objective To notice differences in the style and structure of fiction and non-fiction writing (Y3T1 T18).

- Write a list of text features on the board, e.g. dialogue, diagrams, labels, episodes, past tense verbs, present tense verbs, exclamation marks. Ask the children to write the titles of the texts and find examples of these features. Ask them to group them by fiction and non-fiction.

Observing Do the children recognise that present tense verbs are used in a report or explanation and past tense is used for narration?

Objective To compare a range of story settings, and to select words and phrases that describe scenes (Y3T1 T1).

- Ask the children to skim-read the stories, and note words and phrases that describe each setting.

- Ask: *How do the settings differ? Would the stories be different if the settings were different?*

Observing Do the children re-read the text and scan for key words and phrases? Do they understand how setting affects plot?

Objective To recognise the key differences between prose and playscript, e.g. by looking at dialogue (Y3T1 T5).

- Ask the children to work with a partner, and find characters who speak in **The Wise Chicken** (chicken, cat, duck, dog).
- Ask them to write the characters' names and dialogue in the form of a play.

Observing Do the children omit the reporting clause from the dialogue?

Sentence level work

Objective To observe the basic conventions of speech punctuation (Y3T1 S7).

- Ask the children to choose a page with a conversation from **Kate's Garden** and re-write it with no speech marks or commas, e.g. Look shouted Jo they've grown at last. That's funny said Kate.
- Swap with a partner and correct the punctuation.

Observing Do the children read the paragraph carefully to make sense of it before they begin?

Objective To use verb tenses with increasing accuracy; use past tense consistently for narration (Y3T1 S4).

- Write the following sentences on the board/paper:
  Every seed _____ a tiny plant. (contain)
  A seed _____ a hard coat. (have)
  Through the hole the seed _____ moisture. (get)
  The cat, the duck and the dog _____ in the sunshine and _____.
  (sit) (watch)
  'Sorry,' _____ the cat. (say)
  'I'll have to do it myself,' _____ the chicken. (think)
- Ask the children to fill in the missing verbs.

Observing Do the children think about fiction and non-fiction before choosing the tense to use?

Word level work

Objective To extend the common vocabulary for introducing and concluding dialogue (Y3T1 W19).

Seeds and Grain

- Write these verbs on the board/paper:
    complained, moaned, sighed, muttered, whispered, cried, grumbled, demanded
- Ask the children to read pages 10 to 13 of **Kate's Garden.** Ask: *Can you choose some verbs to replace "said" on these pages?*
- Ask them to read to a partner using the new verbs.

Observing Do the children read with appropriate expression?

Comprehension
Ask the children:
- *What did Kate and Anna do that stopped their seeds from growing?* (p8 They dug them up to look at them.)
- *What three things do seeds need to make them start growing?* (p18 moisture, air and warmth)
- *Why didn't the hungry chicken eat the wheat she found?* (p20 She wanted to grow the wheat to make bread as that would be more food.)
- *Why was the little man named "Red Feather"?* (p31 to represent the corn with a red plume on top of it)

Speaking and listening activities

Objectives Show clear shape and organisation with an introduction and an ending (1d); speak audibly and clearly using spoken standard English in formal contexts (1e).

- Ask children to read **All About Seeds** with a partner, and note key points. Tell them to organise these into a paragraph, and to rehearse giving a short talk with their partners.

Writing

Objective To write simple non-chronological reports from known information e.g. from texts read, using notes made to organise and present ideas. Write for other pupils in class (Y3T1 T23).

- Ask the children to re-write the notes they made for their "talk" into a report using their own words.

◀▶ **Cross-curricular link**
Science: helping plants grow well

Haunted Houses

Before reading

- Look at the front cover with the children and read the title together. Flick through the book and talk about how this is an anthology, with more than one story, unlike many other Oxford Reading Tree books they have read.
- Ask the children about the three texts it contains. Ask the children: *What links these texts?* (ghosts) *What is the main difference?* (Two are stories, one is non-fiction.)

During reading

- Ask the children to read *William and the Ghost* and then *All About Ghosts* and *Miss Terry's Holiday* on separate occasions. Vocabulary that children may need help with includes "battlements" p2; "brooches" p13; "imagination" p16; "mechanic" p30. Praise and encourage them while they read. Prompt as necessary.

Observing Check that the children:
- understand the distinction between fact and fiction; use the terms "fact", "fiction" and "non-fiction" appropriately (Y3T1 T17)
- use an awareness of grammar to decipher new or unfamiliar words (Y3T1 S1).

Group and independent reading activities

Text level work

Objective To express their views about a story, identifying specific words and phrases to support their viewpoint (Y3T1 T8).

- Ask the children to read *William and the Ghost*. Ask: *Can you say what sort of story this is?* (ghost story)
- Ask them in pairs to find words and phrases that help to build up atmosphere (gloomy, secret rooms, lost treasure, disappeared, dark, suddenly, damp tunnel, gasped).

Observing Do the children identify vocabulary typically used in ghost stories?

Objective To understand the distinction between fact and fiction; to use terms "fact", "fiction" and "non-fiction" appropriately (Y3T1 T17).

- Ask the children to read pages 20 and 21. Ask: *How do these pages differ from the other texts in the book?* (non-fiction, present tense verbs, no dialogue)

Observing Do the children recognise the difference between a story and information?

Objective To compare a range of story settings, and to select words and phrases that describe scenes (Y3T1 T1).

- Ask the children to read and compare the two stories, **William and the Ghost** and **Miss Terry's Holiday**, and to write the descriptive vocabulary which describes the settings. Ask: *How do the settings differ?*

Observing Do the children understand that settings affect events?

Sentence level work

Objective To be aware of the function of verbs in sentences through collecting and classifying examples of verbs from reading (Y3T1 S3).

- Discuss the verbs used to describe speech in **William and the Ghost**. Write the following verbs on the board/paper:
    groaned, laughed, whispered, explained, gasped.
- Ask the children to say how these verbs affect the meaning of the speech they relate to, and write similar new spoken words for each.

Observing Do the children recognise that the verbs in reporting clauses indicate how the character feels?

Objective To use commas to separate items in a list (Y3T1 S13).

- Ask the children to read **Miss Terry's Holiday** and write a sentence describing the things she saw in the cottage.

Observing Do the children punctuate their sentence, using capital letters, commas and full stops correctly?

Word level work

Objective To know the convention of how the spellings of verbs alter when –ing is added (Y3T1 W8).

- Ask the children to read page 1 of **William and the Ghost**. Discuss how the consonant is doubled when "swim" becomes "swimming".
- Write the following verbs "visit", "like", "plan" on the board or paper.
- Ask the children to add "–ing" to the verbs and to find two other verbs in the story which follow each of the three patterns (adding "–ing" to the whole word; deleting the "e"; doubling the final consonant).

Haunted Houses

Observing Do the children scan the text to test words to find verbs that fit each pattern?

Comprehension
Ask the children:
- *How did reading the booklet change William's feelings about the visit to Gloomy Castle?* (p3 He became interested in the story of the house.)
- *What evidence is there in the story that tells you William did not dream about the ghost?* (p19 The last picture shows the candlestick from the secret room.)
- *Write two reasons why people tell ghost stories?* (p20 They want to believe in them and they like to scare each other.)
- *Why didn't the little girl in* **"Miss Terry's Holiday"** *know what a phone is?* (p28 Because she was a ghost from before phones were invented.)

Speaking and listening activities

Objectives Make contributions relevant to the topic and take turns in discussion (3a); qualify or justify what they think after listening to others' questions or accounts (3c).

- Ask each child: *Which ghost story do you think is most scary? Why?* Ask them to show evidence from the stories that support their views.

Writing

Objective To develop the use of settings in own stories by writing a description in the style of a familiar story (Y3T1 T11).

- Ask the children to read the descriptions of Gloomy Castle and the cottage, and to write their own descriptions of a spooky setting for a ghost story.

◀▶ **Cross-curricular link**
Music: painting with sound – Exploring sound colours

Seas and Storms

Before reading

- Look at the front cover with the children and read the title together. Flick through the book and talk about how this is an anthology, with more than one story, unlike many other Oxford Reading Tree books they have read.
- Ask the children to flick through the book and talk together about the three texts. Ask the children: *What links these texts?* (rescue at sea) *What is the main difference?* (One is fiction, two are non-fiction.)

During reading

- Ask the children to read the texts on separate occasions. Vocabulary that children may need help with includes "dangerous" p1; "amusement", "dodgems" p3; "lifeguard" p5; "Forfarshire" p26; "jagged" p29; "exhausted" p31. Praise and encourage them while they read. Prompt as necessary.

Observing Check that the children:

- understand the distinction between fact and fiction (Y3T1 T17)
- notice the difference in style and structure of fiction and non-fiction writing (Y3T1 T18).

Group and independent reading activities

Text level work

Objective To understand how dialogue is presented in stories; how paragraphing is used to organise dialogue (Y3T1 T2).

- Prepare a page of dialogue from **Danger At Sea,** writing it as a continuous piece of text, e.g. page 3. Ask: *Where should new lines begin?* (for each new speaker) Ask them to re-write the passage correctly.

Observing Do the children indent the lines to show a change of speaker?

Objective To read information passages, and identify main points or gist of text, by noting key points covered (Y3T1 T21).

- Discuss what the children already know about lighthouses. Write these questions on a board or paper and ask the children to find the answers in the text.

What is the purpose of a lighthouse?
When was the first glass lighthouse lamp invented?
Why are lighthouses painted white?
How are lightvessels different from other ships?

Observing Do the children read from the beginning or scan the text for answers?

Objective To compare the way information is presented (Y3T1 T20).

- Explain that the story of **Grace Darling** is true (non-fiction, recount). Ask the children to find the similarities and differences in the structure and language in the report, **All About Lighthouses**, and the recount (**All About Lighthouses** – headings and subheadings, present tense verbs. **Grace Darling** – past tense, narrative. Both – dates supporting evidence).

Observing Do the children scan the text to find examples?

Sentence level work

Objective To use past tense consistently for narration (Y3T1 S4).

- Write these sentences from **Grace Darling** using present tense verbs.
  On 7th September 1838 Grace wakes up very early.
  There is a terrible storm outside.
  The sea is crashing against the rocks.
  Grace tosses and turns but she can't get back to sleep.
  She gets out of bed and climbs up to the lantern room.
  Grace peers out into the dark.
- Ask the children to re-write the sentences putting the verbs into the past tense.

Observing Do the children write irregular past tenses accurately'? (woke, was, couldn't, got)

Objective To take account of the grammar and punctuation when reading aloud (Y3T1 S2).

- Ask the children to re-read **Danger At Sea** with a partner, taking turns to read a page each aloud using an expressive tone.

Observing Do the children pause at full stops and raise their tone for questions?

Word level work

Objective To discriminate syllables in reading and spelling (Y3T1 W4).

- Ask the children to clap the syllables in "seaside". Explain that this is a compound word made from two smaller words. Remind them that the number of phonemes or letters is not the same as the number of syllables.
- Ask them to scan the book to find other compound words and group them according to the number of syllables (two syllables – breakfast, lifeguard, deckchair, starfish, sideways, lifeboat, inshore, lighthouse, seaweed; three syllables – sandcastle, lifeboatmen, lighthouses, lightvessels, newspapers).

Observing Do the children recognise that the plural of "lighthouse" adds a syllable, but the plural of "lightvessel" stays the same?

Comprehension

Ask the children:
- *What does the red flag mean on the beach?* (p5 It is dangerous to swim.)
- *Why did Mike stop being silly?* (p18 He had a nasty shock.)
- *What is the most important thing about lighthouses?* (p21 They must be easy to see.)
- *How many lives did Grace Darling and her father save?* (p32 nine)

Speaking and listening activities

Objectives Ask relevant questions to clarify, extend and follow up ideas (2b); respond to others appropriately, taking into account what they say (2e); use dramatic techniques to explore characters and issues (4c).

- Ask children to take the role of Grace Darling and sit on the "hot seat". Ask the other children to interview her for a newspaper article.

Writing

Objective To begin to organise stories into paragraphs; to begin to use paragraphing in presentation of dialogue (Y3T1 T16).

- Ask the children to write an imagined conversation between Grace Darling and a shipwreck survivor.

◀▶ **Cross-curricular link**
Geography: weather around the world

Games and Races

Before reading

- Look at the front cover and read the title with the children. Flick through the book and talk about how this is an anthology, with more than one story, unlike many other Oxford Reading Tree books they have read.
- Ask the children to flick through the book and talk together about the texts it contains. Ask the children: *What links these texts?* (competitions and Chinese horoscopes) *What differences are there?* (a story with a modern setting, a non-fiction report, and a myth)

During reading

- Ask the children to read the texts on separate occasions. Vocabulary that children may need help with includes "substitute" p13; "horoscopes" p22; "patience", "honest" p23; "decision" p32. Praise and encourage them while they read. Prompt as necessary.

Observing Check that the children:
- understand the distinction between fact and fiction; use terms "fact", "fiction" and "non-fiction" appropriately (Y3T1 T17)
- take account of grammar and punctuation (Y3T1 S2).

Group and independent reading activities

Text level work

Objective To understand how dialogue is presented, e.g. through statements, questions, exclamations (Y3T1 T2).

- Read the dialogue on page 7 of **The Catch** with the children, "Why are you looking so miserable today, Ben?" "It's no fun just watching," "Nonsense!"
- Ask: *Which is a question, which a statement and which an exclamation?*
- Ask the children to look through the story and collect three more examples of each kind of dialogue.

Observing Do the children look for the punctuation to identify the three kinds of dialogue?

Objective To understand the distinction between fact and fiction; to use terms "fact", "fiction", and "non-fiction" appropriately (Y3T1 T17).

Games and Races   21

- Ask the children to read **Chinese Horoscopes**. Ask: *What kind of text is this?*
- Ask them to identify the features that tell them it is non-fiction (headings, sub-headings, present tense verbs).
- Ask them to find which animal rules the year in which they were born.
- Ask: *Do you need to read the text in the order in which it is written?*

Observing Do the children scan the sub-headings to find their horoscope?

Objective To compare a range of story settings, and to select words and phrases that describe scenes (Y3T1 T1).

- Ask the children to read **The Race**, and make notes of words and phrases that describe the setting. Ask them to select words and phrases that would not be used to describe the setting of an everyday school story.

Observing Do the children understand how language affects setting and style?

Sentence level work

Objective To use verb tenses with increasing accuracy in speaking and writing. Use past tense consistently for narration (Y3T1 S4).

- Ask children to work with a partner and take turns to re-tell **The Race**.

Observing Do the children use the past tense, and vocabulary appropriate to the style of the myth?

Objective To be aware of the function of verbs in sentences through experimenting with changing simple verbs in sentences and discussing their impact on meaning (Y3T1 S3).

- Ask the children to read **Chinese Horoscopes** on page 22.
- Ask them to write a list of the verbs according to singular and plural.
- Ask them to re-write one of the horoscopes, changing the verbs from plural to singular, then swap their writing with a partner and identify what else needs changing to make sense of the sentences.

Observing Do the children change the plural nouns to singular nouns?

Word level work

Objective To practise new spellings regularly by "look, say, cover, write, check" strategy (Y3T1 W7).

- Ask the children to write the list of animals featured in *Chinese Horoscopes* and to practise their spelling using "look, say, cover, write, check".

Observing Do the children practise any words they have difficulty with?

Comprehension

Ask the children:
- *Why did Ben feel miserable on the school Open Day?* (p7 He thought he would only be able to watch.)
- *In what two ways did Father O'Leary help Ben?* (p13 He lent him his collar for fancy dress. He ran when Ben batted.)
- *Which signs in the Chinese horoscope are described as "cheerful"?* (p22 the Rat and, p24, the Horse)
- *Which animal cheated in the race, and how?* (p31 The rat jumped on to the ox's back in the river.)

Speaking and listening activities

Objectives Make contributions relevant to the topic and take turns in discussion (3a); take up and sustain different roles (3e).

- Draw up a list of characteristics from all the Chinese horoscopes for the children to use. Play "Guess who I am". Ask one of the children to choose an animal, and the other children ask questions, e.g. "Are you strong?" The first to guess the animal takes a turn.

Writing

Objective To develop the use of settings in own stories by writing a description in the style of a familiar story (Y3T1 T11).

- Ask the children to write a paragraph describing the setting of *The Race*, using words and phrases from the story.

◀▶ **Cross-curricular link**
Citizenship: taking part – developing skills of communication and participation

Oxford Reading Tree resources at this level

- Glow-worm Poetry Stages 8-9, 10-11, and 11
- Cross Curricular Jackdaws Stage 10, Stage 11
- Oxford Reading Tree True Stories Pack 1, Pack 2,
- Oxford Reading Tree Citizenship Stories
- TreeTops Stories Stage 10 Pack A, Pack C, Stage 11 Pack A, Pack B
- TreeTops True Stories Pack 1
- FireFlies Non-Fiction

OXFORD
UNIVERSITY PRESS

Great Clarendon Street, Oxford OX2 6DP

Oxford University Press is a department of the University of Oxford. It furthers the University's objective of excellence in research, scholarship, and education by publishing worldwide in

Oxford   New York

Auckland Cape Town Dar es Salaam Hong Kong Karachi
Kuala Lumpur Madrid Melbourne Mexico City Nairobi
New Delhi Shanghai Taipei Toronto

With offices in

Argentina Austria Brazil Chile Czech Republic France Greece
Guatemala Hungary Italy Japan Poland Portugal Singapore
South Korea Switzerland Thailand Turkey Ukraine Vietnam

Oxford is a registered trade mark of Oxford University Press
in the UK and in certain other countries

© Oxford University Press 2004

The moral rights of the author have been asserted

Database right Oxford University Press (maker)

First published 2004

All rights reserved. No part of this publication may be reproduced, stored in a retrieval system, or transmitted, in any form or by any means, without the prior permission in writing of Oxford University Press, or as expressly permitted by law, or under terms agreed with the appropriate reprographics rights organization. Enquiries concerning reproduction outside the scope of the above should be sent to the Rights Department, Oxford University Press, at the address above

You must not circulate this book in any other binding or cover and you must impose this same condition on any acquirer

British Library Cataloguing in Publication Data

Data available

Cover artwork by Nick Harris

Teacher's Notes: ISBN 978-0-19-845455-7

10 9 8 7

Page make-up by IFA Design Ltd, Plymouth, Devon

Printed in China by Imago